An Angel

Named

Santa

A Story About Real Life

NELL F. SEVISON

AuthorHouse™
1663 Liberty Drive
Bloomington, IN 47403
www.authorhouse.com
Phone: 1 (800) 839-8640

Published by AuthorHouse 08/15/2018

ISBN: 978-1-5462-5584-0 (sc)
ISBN: 978-1-5462-5586-4(hc)
ISBN: 978-1-5462-5585-7(e)

Print information available on the last page.

authorHOUSE®

NIV Hebrews 13:2 -"Don't neglect to show hospitality, for by doing this some have welcomed angels as guests without knowing it."

CHRISTMAS 1983

An Angel Named Santa
A Story About Real Life
By
Nell F. Sevison

"The First Christmas," 1983. In everyone's life, at one point or another, there are events that are so overwhelming that good, bad, or otherwise, they are committed to memory forever. Well, Christmas 1983 was like that for me. It was good, bad, *and* otherwise. Ultimately, it was the beginning of a seven-year adventure that – at the very least – should be called awesome! My husband was in the service; we had been married for 18 years and had three children. Our separation couldn't have come at a more inopportune time.

It was a horrible time. The children and I had moved off Base and were living "hand-to-mouth." I was working 16 hours a week at the local newspaper, but had not been able to find anything fulltime, fortunately, because of my contacts with local realtors through my job, I found a house to rent that was very cheap. I ironed for people, babysat, cleaned houses, and anything else I could to provide for the kids.

As Christmas approached, it was not a season to be jolly. It was in fact, dreadful in every conceivable way. Up to this point I didn't even go to church regularly, so my view of Christmas was very materialistic. The week before Christmas I had $70.00 to spend on a tree, gifts for three kids, *and* Christmas dinner. To make matters even more difficult, my mother decided to come spend the holidays with us. Mom was living on a very limited income herself and I knew that she would worry, so I hadn't told her what life was really like for us and she had no idea how we were living. Now to make things even worse, I would have to make everything seem "fine".

Things weren't fine; in fact, things couldn't get much worse. On December 24th, mom and I went shopping. I told her that the kids and I had decided to go back to an "old fashioned" Christmas. We were only going to use homemade decorations and no lights. Mom believed it, and when I told her I didn't have the tree yet, because I hadn't had time off of work to go get one, she believed that, too. I felt awful lying to her! I didn't lie when I was a child, and I had always heard that once you tell one lie, it leads to another and another and so on. Well, it's true.

I had been able to get each of the kids just one gift, and by the time we went to bed on Christmas eve, our "Charley Brown" tree had been decorated, and it seemed like I might actually be able to pull this off. Then my mom said something, I don't even remember what, but I knew that she thought there were other gifts for the kids and that I was going to "play" Santa. I realized very quickly that when morning came she would figure out the truth and then she would really be upset. She would be very hurt that I hadn't told her and even more, she would be very sad for the kids. *What a mess!!*

I couldn't sleep, so I finally got up and went into the living room and sat in the dark. The house we lived in was at the end of a street that had no street lights, and it had been very cloudy all day; even now I could hear the sound of a gentle rain on the roof. In front of me I could barely make out the silhouette of the tree, and next to it was a small, two-level table with our nativity set on the top and the family Bible opened to the story of Christmas in the book of Matthew. I became aware of a dusty kind of light streaming in through the window. It was strange, because it seemed to be coming from left to right, shining directly on the nativity and yet the tree didn't block any of the light. I glanced up at the window and wondered where the light was coming from. It didn't seem to have any origin, it wasn't all that bright, and yet... there it was! When I looked at the nativity again I was suddenly flooded with emotions. It's as if for the first time in my life I really understood the *true* meaning of Christmas. In just that one moment of time, I could see that it wasn't about gifts, and trees and meals. It didn't even have anything to do with me. I felt so guilty and so very sorry that all I had done this season was to feel sorry for myself and my family because we couldn't have all the "stuff" everyone else had. If only I could take it all back! I started to pray – *really* pray. I wanted to tell God that I was sorry for my selfishness, sorry for not remembering. I don't know how long I was on my knees, but when I finished, the house was again dark, the rain still sprinkled softly on the roof, and everything was as it had been. Everything...except *me!*

I went back to bed, still feeling a little sad that my children weren't going to have a great Christmas, but I knew that somehow it was going to be alright. I had finally drifted off to sleep when suddenly I heard a noise on the roof above me. It sounded like rustling, and at first I thought it was the wind brushing a tree branch across the roof. I started to fall asleep again, but awoke with a start, realizing that I didn't have a tree on that side of the house! I got up, made a quick check of the house, and finding that all was well, again went back to bed. Mom was still sleeping peacefully, so I decided I must have dreamed the noise.

Sometime before I fell into a deep sleep, I again heard something on the roof! This time it was a very loud thud. I got up and carefully went through the entire house. It was so dark I couldn't even see anything out the windows. I didn't hear anything else; the family dog didn't bark or seem restless. I decided that I had just been dreaming again. As I headed back to bed my daughter spoke from behind me and ask what the loud noise was. Part of me was elated that someone else had heard the noise and part of me was really puzzled about what it was. I explained that I didn't know what the noise was, but I had checked everything very well and all was okay: Grandma was still asleep, Snowball wasn't barking, so we should just go back to bed. Then, Amy looked past me and asked where the light in the front window was coming from. When I turned around, I saw the same strange, hazy light I had seen earlier, only now it wasn't coming in the window, but rather shining across the front of the house! We both went to the font of the living room. I tried to see where the light was coming from and again it didn't seem to have an origin. It did, however, stop at the front door, and as I looked out I could see something shining. Amy opened the door and the whole front porch was full of gifts!

I was sure that the gifts were left for someone else - a previous tenant perhaps. I didn't think we should even handle them, but Amy reminded me that it was still sprinkling rain and they would get soaked if we left them outside. As she brought them in, she shuffled through the tags; then she began to read them out loud. These gifts were for us! The tags all were signed, *"Santa."*

By now everyone was up and the living room was suddenly transformed into a hub of excitement. We began to open the gifts. There were four gifts for each child and four for me. There were also two gifts for my mother. The kids and I each got a set of towels – navy blue for Matthew, light blue for David, dusty rose for me and pink for Amy. We also got a small decorative gift with money in it: five dollars for each child, twenty dollars for me.

I knew by my mother's reaction that she was genuinely surprised, and she was also sure that I had planned all this out very carefully. Her reaction immediately eliminated her from the possibilities of who *did* plan the "Great Santa Mystery."

Aside from the events leading up to finding the gifts, and discovering that they were for us, I noted that there were other oddities. The first was, *"Why us?"* and *"Why this particular Christmas?"* I was a very private person, and my pride was a major factor of my personality. I hadn't told anyone about the situation we were in. I was the only one who knew the circumstances of this Christmas.

The second strange thing was my mother's gifts: they were different from ours. They were very appropriate for her and wrapped in a different paper. It wasn't necessarily holiday wrap, and it was a shade of what we now call "country" blue. Blue was her favorite color, especially *that* blue. Mother even getting gifts at my house was also strange, especially since she hadn't decided to spend Christmas at my house until just a few days before. She called the airlines and surprisingly found a flight that had one seat open and she took it. I didn't know she was coming until December 22. I had already gotten off work for the holidays so I

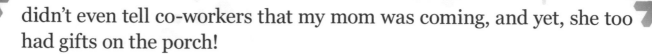

didn't even tell co-workers that my mom was coming, and yet, she too had gifts on the porch!

My next thought was that maybe my sister, was our "Santa"; however, it wasn't long before I discounted her. She knew mom was at my house, and she did know the age and gender of my children, BUT, she had never been to Twentynine Palms, she didn't know anyone here, so how could she have staged the delivery? I called her first thing Christmas morning to wish her a happy day, and also to find out if she was there at her home. She was!

After calling my family, I went outside to survey the driveway in front of the house. It was a circular drive that was all dirt. Since it had sprinkled all night, I was sure I would see some tire tracks. There were no tracks in the drive or in the street at either end of the drive. (I have *no* idea what difference it would have made if I *had* found tracks!)

It was a wonderful day! So filled with Christmas magic... My mom, my kids, and anyone I eventually told about the visit from "Santa" were convinced that I had planned everything. After all, I'm really the only one who knew all the details needed to pull it off. You see, the clothing was just the right size, the "fun" gift was really fun for the one that received it, the colors matched each person's own taste, and of course there were those two gifts for my mom.

Only *I* know just how full of magic that Christmas was!

December, 1984. The sweet memories of last year's magical Christmas now offered a haven for a saddened soul and a troubled heart.

After that most amazing day in 1983, Mom, the kids and I went to Pasadena to watch the Rose Parade. It was an exhausting adventure, but we all agreed that everyone should go in person at least once in their lifetime. We, on the other hand, had gone our one time, and it was now our "educated choice" to watch it from the comfort of our own living room in the future! When we arrived home that evening it seemed that my mom was unusually tired. She was older, yes, but had stayed fairly active, and wasn't in the habit of taking daily naps. This seemed to be more than just "tired."

I went back to work on January 2nd. When I got home the kids said that "Grams" had been in bed all day. I checked on her and she was o.k., but still very, very tired. The next day was pretty much the same, except now when she was awake or trying to talk, she was very emotional. She seemed to be very depressed and "weepy". On January 4th I returned home from work to find mom packing her suitcases. She said that she was "just in the way" and rambled something about "bothering the kids". I was sure that one of the kids had said something that she either didn't hear correctly or misunderstood. The kids adored her and would have liked her to live with us.

When I ask the kids what had happened they collectively had no idea what I was talking about. Amy, the oldest, said, "Grandma has been asleep all day, just like the last two days. She didn't even come out of the bedroom." This was really unusual behavior! I went back to talk to her and she was very, very agitated and determined to leave that night. I called my sister and we decided that maybe coming home was a good idea, so I booked a flight for the next day. When she left on the 5th, Mom was very quiet. She didn't seem "upset" anymore, but her fatigue was really worrying me. She even needed assistance to board the plane.

The remainder of that day after she returned home, Mom slept in her own bed, where she also remained the next day. My sister went over at noon the following day and found that Mom had fallen. She took Mom to the doctor and she seemed to be fine, but the very next day, she fell again and this time was hospitalized with a broken pelvis. On the second day after admittance, Mom suffered what appeared to be a mild stroke. Though her speech was garbled, her motor responses on both sides were fine. Before long, however, Mom slipped into a very deep depression and totally lost her will to live. She never went home again. Soon she was transferred to a care facility and in June, she died.

Mother's passing left such a tremendous void in all our lives.

For the kids it must have seemed even worse. They had "lost" their dad and now their "Grams." In September the house we were renting sold and we had to move; another loss for them. Fortunately, thanks in part to realtor connections, I found a small three bedroom house not very far away - on a corner, two blocks from where I worked, and just down the street from the fire station. The change helped, but there was still something missing.

Sometime in November, I decided to sell my piano and use the money to fly home with the kids. They adored their Aunt, and they always loved being around their cousins. The excitement of going home did the trick. It's all the kids talked about.

November 30th was the best day of all. My piano sold and I would be getting our tickets the next day. I had a doctor's appointment near the airport and I was planning to "pop" over and pick up the tickets.

The next day, Amy came by work to pick me up. She was going to go with me, and after my appointment, we were going to do some "girl stuff" at the mall. As we were leaving the newspaper office, the scanner went off. *"TC with injuries; corner of Buena Vista and Lupine."* Calls like this were common place at the paper. When the scanner toned, the reporters would grab cameras; one of us would copy the address, and then hand it to whoever was on the way out the door. *Nothing different about this* – except, an eerie feeling. I felt a chill, and a sense of panic. I almost cancelled our plans for the afternoon, the feeling was that strong. I decided that I was just tired, and the impending trip home, although exciting, was kind of stressful for me.

We left for Palm Springs as planned, and I shared my feelings of "impending disaster" with Amy. She reminded me that her brothers were safe and sound at school, and that there wasn't anyone else to worry about. *She was right, of course.*

When we arrived at the doctor's office the receptionist told me that I needed to come in back and call work immediately. She asked if the girl with me was Amy, and when I told her it was, she said she needed to call a family friend. Amy was on one phone, and I was on the other. My boss told me not to panic, but my son had been in an auto accident. I don't remember a lot of what he said after that point, except, I couldn't get him to tell me which son. David was nine and attended elementary school, and Matthew was 16 and was in high school. <u>Both</u> *should have been* in school!

Amy and I finished our calls at the same time, and then raced to the car, exchanging information. He was taken to Hi Desert Hospital in Joshua Tree. Amy had also found out it was Matthew.

When I arrived at the hospital I signed the necessary consent papers and was able to see Matthew. He didn't look too bad. A few scrapes, but nothing really serious. He would have X-rays and then probably be released.

In the waiting room we were able to piece together what happened. Matthew and his friend had left campus in the friend's car. They went to a local burger shop and were on their way back to school. After stopping at a four-way stop sign, they proceeded into an intersection, where their car was broadsided on Matthew's side by a large van.

It didn't take long to figure out: Looks can be so deceiving! Matthew's injuries turned out to be monumental. After three days in intensive care it was decided that Matthew would be air-lifted to the trauma center at Balboa Naval Hospital in San Diego.

Within hours of our arrival in San Diego, Matthew was taken into surgery. The prognosis was grave. The surgery would be done by "teams" starting with the most serious injury. Matthew had a 2-inch tear in his aorta, which required cardiac surgery. The surgery was ended after 15 hours. The aorta was repaired and internal bleeding was stopped, but the orthopedic team could only stabilize his crushed pelvis. Since both of his lungs had been punctured Matthew went into surgery with pneumonia and added time under anesthetic was not an option. Matthew was on a respirator in the Intensive Care unit for 21 days following the surgery. It was questionable whether he would ever walk again.

My sister had come within hours of the accident. She stayed for two weeks, alternating her time between the hospital with me and Twentynine Palms with Amy and David. On December 17th she returned to San Jose and on December 20th Amy and David joined her.

After the other kids went to their aunt's house, I was able to stay with Matthew constantly, but I was also torn emotionally. While it was easier for me to focus on Matthew, I knew that Amy and David were basically alone, worrying about their brother and missing their mom.

On December 21, Matthew was taken off the respirator and moved into the "step down" unit. On December 23rd the doctors told us that if I could arrange to have the proper hospital equipment at home, and provide non-sitting transportation, Matthew could go home for Christmas! The only other condition was that he would have to be re-admitted on December 26.

The outpouring of love and support of our community was fantastic! I called the paper, who in turn called the radio station, and when I got to Twentynine Palms that afternoon, all the necessary equipment was waiting to be delivered! By 6:00 pm December 23rd, everything was in place. At 7:00 am the following morning, a van with a mattress in the back was dropped off, and by 9:00 am I was on my way back to San Diego. It was unbelievable!

It felt *so* good to bring Matthew home! We arrived around dinner time on the 24th. Since we lived directly down the street from the fire station, when the firemen saw us pull up, they came down and carried Matthew into the house.

Matt and I decided that we would postpone Christmas dinner until we were all together again as a family. We didn't have much in the house to eat, but neither one of us was very hungry anyway. It was enough to be together and know that Matthew was alive and would someday be okay again!

The front of our house was mostly glass. The dining room and living room were really one long rectangular room. Each room had its own window facing front, but each also had a side window, allowing visibility of the entire front of the house. The front door located between the two rooms was a full length window-paned door. Our dining room had been transformed into Matthew's temporary "hospital" room.

I slept on the couch a few feet from Matthew's bed. In the morning passing the front door, I checked on Matthew and went into the kitchen. When I came back to his bedside, I noticed something on the front porch. I opened the door and there was a huge box. The box was the size of a small refrigerator. It was entirely wrapped in Christmas paper, with a note that simply read, *"for Nell and Matthew from Santa."*

The box was *so* big and *so* full I had to unload more than half before I could drag it into the house! Matthew was watching in wonder as I unloaded everything needed to make an awesome Christmas dinner. There was even food to stock the pantry! As I tipped the box to drag it into the house, I could see that there were wrapped Christmas gifts in the box also. I looked at them and there were six gifts: three for Matthew and three for me.

As Matthew opened his first gift, slippers and socks, I was filled with a warm feeling of love. Love from a community, or so I thought. When Matt opened the second gift, the warm feeling gave way to an eerie feeling of déjà vu. The second gift was a small leather organizer with $5.00 in it. I handed him the third gift and was speechless when he opened a set of towels. Brown and tan with ducks on them - obviously towels for a man/boy. Matthew was beside himself! He, too, saw the connection to the previous Christmas and couldn't wait for me to open my gifts. I had a personal gift for me, a decorative gift for the house which was the right color and also contained $20.00, and, can you guess? *A set of towels!* This set of towels was shades of pastel green. So was the bathroom in this house!

Coincidence? Maybe, but the common factors seemed almost too odd to be chance. As with the first year, the "Santa" note and the name tags were made up of cut-out letters pasted and taped to paper. Matthew and I received three gifts each, of which one contained the same amount of money as the year before, and we each got a set of towels as we had the year before.

As I had the year before, I tried every avenue I could think of to track down "our Santa." Every time I investigated a new idea, it led to a dead end. Some sort of glitch that couldn't be explained away. I knew for a positive fact that it was not someone in my family. Community? Charitable organization? Perhaps... but how could they know sizes, colors, preferences, and the color of my bathroom or that it had changed since last year? And how on earth did *whoever* get that big box unloaded on my front porch without waking Matthew, me, or our dog? Do we know this person? Even so, Buffie would definitely have barked.

So many unanswered questions.

Is there really a Santa Claus?

December, 1985. Compared to the prior two years, 1985 was a breeze!

My little family and I were holding our own. My job at the paper had gone to 40 hours a week, which meant I could give up my other two part time jobs. We weren't living on "Easy Street" but nonetheless, we were making it.

Amy was almost 18, a senior in high school. She had a steady beau. He was quite a bit older than Amy and not my choice for her, but she seemed happy enough.

Matthew was 17 now and well on the mend from the accident. He was walking by the end of January, just two months after that horrific day, and he returned to school the end of May. Matt would never play competitive sports again, but considering the other possibilities he faced it seemed a small price to pay. It certainly didn't dampen his enthusiasm! Other than the surgical scars which were covered by his clothing, and the medic alert tag he wore because of the aortic graft, there were no outward reminders.

David was almost 11 and doing well in school. He was starting to be a little competitive with Matthew, which was good. All in all it seemed like we were finally back to normal.

As Christmas approached, we decided that Amy's beau would stay over Christmas Eve and share Christmas day with our family. As we decorated the tree, the kids had great fun telling Amy's beau all about *"Our Santa."* Sometime between last year and now, the story seemed to morph into some kind of cross between an Ellery Queen mystery and a Stephen King fantasy. All tragedy past, the kids were now sure it was very supernatural! Amy's beau, on the other hand, was not convinced. Being somewhat skeptical, but not wanting to get on Amy's bad side, he went along with the story as if it were "gospel."

As Christmas Eve approached, Amy's beau thought up an elaborate plan to catch "Santa." We were all going to take shifts in twos and post

guards at the windows. It was all great fun, and although I wasn't sure about how I really felt, I went along with it. Part of me wondered if it really was Our Santa, and if it was, did I really want to catch him? The other part of me, my more logical side, maintained that there was a rational explanation for the similarities and there really wasn't any magic at all. In all probability, it was a coincidence and it wouldn't happen this year anyway.

Well, the old saying starts, "the best laid plans..." I don't know which two had this particular "shift," but we all fell asleep. Amy and I were in our rooms at the back of the house, David and Amy's beau were in the living room/dining room and I'm not sure where Matthew was. All of a sudden, we were awakened by what sounded like a "wedding party: car horns pierced the night like an intruder. We all headed for the closest window, but not one of us saw a single car. We collaborated in the living room for a few minutes and decided that at the very least, we had heard *two* car horns. We looked at the clock and it was 2:00 a.m. About that time, the kids turned to look at me and I at them, and in a sudden frenzy we all headed for the front door. As we opened the front door the whole yard seemed to sparkle, just like a Currier & Ives painting! The evergreen trees were covered with spray snow, as was the yard. "Merry Christmas" was sprayed in snow across the sidewalk and the front porch was filled with gifts. As it had been the two preceding years, there was a note to me – cut out letters pasted on a piece of paper, which read, *"Merry Christmas, from Santa."* The name tags also simply read, *"from Santa."*

As in the previous two years, the kids and I each received three gifts. All clothing was the right size and color. We each got something with money in it, and we each got a set of towels: navy for Matthew, light blue for David, dusty rose for Amy, and yellow & orange for me. Yes, my bathroom had changed colors that year!

What about Amy's beau? He received two gifts, both wrapped in masculine paper, and both appropriate for an adult man.

Now there wasn't *any* question! This was no coincidence!

Determined to find out who the mysterious Santa was, I followed through on any and all suggestions, and leads we had. Some were seemingly silly, but I checked them out. Even though I seemed to be hot on the trail at times, sooner or later I would run into a complete dead end. The most exasperating part was that as time passed, even possibilities faded. We changed addresses. Living in a military town alone lent itself to complete and total changes in circles of friends. This was true for both the kids and me.

Oh, well... Next year we'll be ready!

December, 1986 – The Fourth Year. 1986 was a quiet year for us. Considering some of the tragedies and disasters that plagued our little family in the past, any event that wasn't monumental was regarded as "normal."

All three kids were doing well in school. Amy was working as a lifeguard during the summer and planned to enroll at California Baptist College (CBC) in Riverside after graduation.

Matthew was having somewhat of a hard time with school. After his re-entry following the accident he had a difficult time finding his "place." Before, he was one of the better athletes and quite a ladies' man. He was easy-going and happy most of the time. This year, we discovered his home study credit had not gotten posted to his files. The counselor had not taken time to look closely at Matthew's records and it was also noted that Matthew had not gotten all of his required classes in. The outcome was that Matt had to attend summer school before and after his senior year, carrying a full credit load all three sessions. To make matters worse, most of Matt's friends were still active in sports, something Matthew couldn't do anymore. Nevertheless, he continued to hang in, and for the most part was doing okay.

David was kind of "coming of age." He would be an official teenager next March, and he seemed to be practicing already! He, like Amy, seemed to be a natural at school work – when he applied himself. This was a year that he applied himself.

I was promoted to office manager at the newspaper. It didn't advance me financially, but it did make my position somewhat more secure.

Once again, our rental house sold and we had to move. The new house was great fun. It had a swimming pool, totally enclosed back yard, and a great patio. We really enjoyed this house! Unfortunately it, too, sold, and after only five months, we moved again.

As Christmas approached, almost all conversations in our house either started with or ended with Our Santa. We were very determined to catch Our Santa in the act, and thus find out once and for all who was behind it. Since there were no major happenings to divert our attentions, we had a lot of time to think about a "perfect plan."

Amy and her beau were still seeing each other and I invited him to partake once again in our holiday plans. Since he had witnessed Our Santa in action last year, he was more than eager!

We actually sat down, all five of us – including Amy's beau, and had strategy meetings. After discussing several different plans, we decided that the previous year "watch" strategy was still the best bet.

Christmas Eve arrived and we were set! We each had an assigned room. The plan was to have two people awake, each helping the other to stay awake. Team 1 would be responsible for waking Team 2 and posting them at their assigned area. It was all very intriguing, and a more dedicated group you could not find. It was great fun!

The sun came up Christmas morning, the sky was blue, the temperature was crisp and a light frost covered the yard. "Operation Santa" had been a total success. Or had it?

While it was true that someone was awake all night, and the assigned teams were successful in watching the windows, nobody saw or heard a thing! This fact seemed to hit all of us at the same time, and we almost tripped over each other getting to the front door. I was reminded of the line in *The Night Before Christmas* that says, *"(he) tore open the shutters, and threw up the sash..."* But to our astonishment, we found the front porch empty! We immediately checked the side door, then the back. It was true. Our Santa hadn't come this year. A subtle, unspoken sadness began to fill the house, like a fog rolling across the land. Disappointment was written on each face. It wasn't the gifts we missed; in fact, it wasn't even the anticipation of *getting* gifts. It was the *magic,* I think it was *always* the mystery of it all.

Even so, we went on to celebrate the Day. We exchanged gifts, went to church, and ate a wonderful dinner together. But somehow it just wasn't quite the same. Somehow, something wonderful that none of us had any right to count on or depend on, had become a tradition. Now it was gone. It was as if a part of us was missing.

Since Christmas fell on a Sunday that year, the next day was a work day for me. I had asked Amy's beau to stay one more night to help with the toy assembly in my absence. I awoke a little late, and having to curtail my usual morning rush to accommodate a guest in the house only made me that much more late. As I rushed through the usual morning frenzy, I couldn't help thinking about *Our Santa.*

Why did it ever start, and why did it stop? I knew it would be the center of conversation as soon as I got to work. By now, my Santa stories were becoming a bit of a legend. Everyone who knew us loved to share in the magic. I truly think that what they loved even more was trying to figure who was behind it. I didn't mind sharing with anyone, though it was somewhat annoying going through the list of "thought of that, checked that, couldn't be," but occasionally someone would suggest something I had overlooked and it gave me a new path to track. Now, the magic was gone, ending as suddenly and unexpectedly as it had started.

Lost in thought, I still managed to pull things together and if I hurried, I would only be a few minutes late. Everyone was still asleep; that was great. No lost minutes in good-byes. I yanked open the side door, rushed through it and promptly found myself on my knees in the drive-way. Reality sunk in pretty quickly. As I rubbed my throbbing knees, I looked up to see what I had tripped over. Can you ever imagine?

On the back step, and down the driveway lay several wonderfully wrapped Christmas packages! I limped back inside and called work. I needed to tell them, *I would be late!*

Heading back outside, I collected the packages. Though I could see a portion of a note, I couldn't read what it said; however, the now-familiar cut-out letters pasted and taped on a piece of paper were all I needed to see! I could feel excitement and anticipation welling up within. What started out to be a gentle call to wake the kids, turned out to be a horrendous scream.

As the kids, and Amy's beau, ran to the dining room, I could see the expressions on their faces change from anger and/or fear, to a most delightful childish glow of excitement. One glance at the stack of presents, and they knew who they were from.

As we examined the gifts, just as in previous years, each of the kids and I received three. You guessed it: a set of towels, something personal, and a decorative gift with $10.00 for each child and $40.00 for me. Amy's beau, although he normally wouldn't have been there the next day, also received a gift.

I started my "Santa-search" again with renewed determination. The path was the same, and so were the clues. Although we now belonged to a church and attended regularly, we didn't have any of the same friends. We had changed addresses not once, but *twice* this past year! I had eliminated my family from the beginning. Even though sister had now

been to Twentynine Palms to visit, and now knew some of my friends, she was raising two kids alone, and financially could not have done it. Of those who could have managed it financially, I/we didn't know them that well, *or* I/we didn't know them in the beginning. (Even Amy's beau didn't come into the picture until the 3rd year.) Nothing was consistent.

All clues led to the same dead end. In four years, the only absolute that was determined was that Our Santa knew almost everything about each of us, knew where we lived, and knew who would be with us on Christmas morning. So this year really *was* different. It reminded me that *nothing* is forever, that our minds can't always wrap themselves around the things we don't fully understand, and that we don't always know "the plan." Sometimes I think "Our Santa" knew our Christmas plans even before I did!

Incidentally, thinking back, when the family responded to my cry from the driveway, Matthew was the last to see what was going on. His face was expressionless, but suddenly his eyes danced. In a quiet, barely audible voice he said, "Dude! *Our Santa* is back!"

Dude, that about says it all!

December 1987. Of all our Christmas stories, that very first year is my most favorite, but it is followed very closely by Christmas 1987.

This year saw a lot of changes at our house. To begin with, *for one whole year we hadn't moved!* Actually, for clarity, I should say that David (my youngest) and I hadn't moved; yet, other changes had occurred in our family dynamic.

Amy was away at college. She had met some new friends, severed her relationship with her beau, and was becoming quite independent. She kind of wanted to make her own holiday plans, and although it meant our first Christmas apart, I felt she was a young woman now, and we both needed to start "growing up."

Matthew had also left home. He was living in South Carolina with his dad and working full time at a commercial nursery. Since he had not been at his job for a full year, coming home for Christmas was not possible. That left just David and me.

I finally had an opportunity to get my old Nova serviced and tuned up, and according to the mechanic, it was road-worthy enough to make the 480-mile trip to my sister Mary's in San Jose. David and I were going "home" for Christmas!

It was a wonderful time for David and me. We hadn't seen our San Jose family for a very long time. The thought of going home was equally exciting for both of us. Our Santa seemed to have gotten lost in all the trip plans. I thought briefly about "him" a few times, but with Amy and Matthew grown and gone, it just seemed to be a part of the past, and even that was "O-kay." (Those who know me well know that little word, said that particular way, was my concession to reality...my peaceful resignation with "how things were.")

David and I agreed that we weren't even going to get a tree or put out many decorations. We had a 6 ft. plant stand with shelves on it. We decorated it and even put lights and tinsel on it. We loved it! We called it our "Christmas Pole."

I was still office manager at the paper, and everything at work was going really well. Late in the year we got a new editor and he was a pleasant, fun loving man. However, as the holidays approached, his attitude began to change. He became very quiet and seemed to be in another world a lot of the time. When the office conversation turned to Christmas, it was very apparent that he wasn't into Christmas, Jesus, or for that matter anything having to do with the Season. I assumed his attitude had something to do with sad memories of past holidays and tried to keep the conversations light, but it was inevitable that my "Santa" story would come up. One slow day a co-worker asked me what I thought Our Santa was going to do this year. Knowing that he was behind the partition I tried to change the subject, but it was not to be. Another fairly new reporter got curious and wanted to know the whole story. I touched on some of the high points, brought it up to the current year, and ended by saying that I wanted to write a story about it.

The following day, he and I had "lunch watch" together. We were the only people in the office and his curiosity was definitely getting the best of him. At first he made a few off-handed remarks about overhearing the Santa story the day before. When I didn't volunteer any information, he asked several probing questions. I knew he was very inquisitive, and I was having fun intentionally withholding any more than he asked about our "legend."

I don't know whether the motivation was curiosity or aggravation, but he eventually couldn't stand it any longer. He burst around the partition, cleared the corner of my desk, sat down, and demanded I tell him "the whole Santa story, with all the details!" It was great fun. I knew by his reaction that he fully intended to solve the mystery. There he sat, notebook in hand, basking in his great investigative abilities. There I sat, knowing without a doubt that he wasn't going to get *anywhere!*

I started from the beginning, and as I recounted the events of the previous years, he took copious notes. I found myself giving him more details than I had recounted at any one time before. Now, I respected his abilities as a "detective," but my real admiration was for his writing skills. I had read some of his creative writings, and he could paint a picture with words. He was one of the most gifted writers I have ever read! My hope was that he would help *write* my story.

When I finished, he gave me some ideas on possible leads I could check out. I had to hand it to him, he did come up with some new ideas not previously explored. Over the next several days he also continued to ask questions, and for clarification of details. I knew the story was churning in his head and he was not going to just dismiss it as coincidence.

As it happened, the day before I was to leave for San Jose, he and I were again sharing lunch break. He asked me how my leads were panning out, and I told him I had followed each one, but again they all led to the same dead end. He was completely exasperated and said, "Fine! I'll tell you what. If "your Santa" shows up in San Jose, then by God, I'll believe!"

My reaction to his statement was surprising. My whole body was engulfed with feelings. It was almost eerie. *Could it happen in San Jose? Could Our Santa possibly find us there? No...that would be impossible! That* was 480 miles from home, and anyway nobody knew what my sister's last name was. Her phone was unlisted, and she lived in a rented house, which meant there would be little chance of discovering the actual owner. Even if someone *(Santa?)* knew my sister's name and the town she lived in, it would be like finding a needle in a haystack. You see, my sister's name is a very common name, and the town is actually a city almost the size of Los Angeles.

David and I arrived in San Jose the evening of December 22nd. The next day was lost in a flurry of activity. David and his cousin went in one direction doing shopping and running errands. My sister and I went in the other direction with our own "To-do" list.

My sister and I had planned Christmas Eve day very well. We would finish up baking, giftwrapping etc. by mid to late afternoon. We would have our traditional Christmas Eve meal of oyster stew, then we would visit until about 10:00 pm. We were planning to attend the midnight service at our "family" church (...meaning the church we went to on special occasions, and the preacher we used for weddings, funerals etc.). We both liked the minister of this church, but since we weren't in regular attendance, we hadn't seen him for a few years.

The morning of the 24th started off just as we had planned it. In fact, most of the day went according to plan, but early in the afternoon things started to deteriorate. She had neglected to get a gift for her brother and had to leave for the mall. David was supposed to spend the day with his cousin Dallas, but Dallas got sick. Just as we were putting the finishing touches on the dressing and getting ready to start the oyster stew, we realized neither one of us had remembered the oysters! (Oysters, incidentally, are a hot item at Christmas time and if you don't get what you want early, you don't get what you want period!) We had to settle for canned oysters, and as if that weren't bad enough, I called the church to inquire about midnight service and found out that there wasn't going to be one! In fact, our beloved Reverend had retired and didn't even live in the area anymore! We were not exactly in a festive mood.

After dinner things did pick up for awhile. My sister's friend, dropped in with the world's all-time best cheesecake. Ordinarily, her cheesecake is very good, but following oyster stew that wasn't up to par, that cheesecake was awesome!

We sat around the kitchen table eating cheesecake and visiting. She asked me to re-tell the now-famous Santa story; she loved to hear it. So we passed the time sharing our tale of happy coincidences from an unknown source.

We were cleaning up the kitchen and feeling melancholy again. Cheesecake is a great pick-me-upper, but it doesn't last long! No church on Christmas Eve just didn't seem right! I suddenly recalled the events preceding that first Santa Christmas. The Nativity and the true meaning of Christmas. I suggested that after the chores were done, we could gather around the organ. I would read the story of Christ's birth according to the Gospel of Matthew, and she could play, and we would sing. Afterward we could pile in the car and drive around looking at lights and decorations. Just because the there was no minister with us and we weren't in a church building didn't mean we couldn't worship the Lord! After all, it was *His* Birthday! Actually, it was really special celebrating with just family. David hadn't been really enthusiastic about the substitution at first, but he really enjoyed having our own "midnight" service.

We left to tour the neighborhood about nine o'clock, and arrived back about an hour and a half later to find a large box on her front porch. It really didn't strike me as a big deal; She had ordered a handmade gift that was guaranteed to be delivered in time for Christmas. UPS would be running until midnight, so I just assumed that's what the box was.

The box was situated on the front porch right next to the door. My sister was the first one to get to it, while I deliberately stalled so she could retrieve the gift and take it inside. She stared at the box and suddenly a very strange look spread over her face. I couldn't understand why she didn't just take the box in the house. She wasn't to be held back any longer and headed for the door. She looked at the box, looked back at me and said, "It's for you!" Now, I was *really* confused! David was next up the sidewalk. He looked at the box, busted out in laughter and exclaimed, "Oh, RAD!!" By this time I was almost to the front porch and couldn't take my eyes off the box. As I got closer to the door I caught sight of what appeared to be peach-colored terry cloth. The same kind of terry cloth that towels are made of! Whatever this peach bundle was, it had a big red ribbon around it. As I drew closer I could see that the peach bundle was, in fact, towels, and underneath were wrapped gifts. At the very bottom of the box I could see the corner of a piece of paper and what looked like a cut-out "S"!

David brought the box inside and with all the zeal of youth, proceeded to unpack it: Three gifts for him, three gifts for me, a gift for my sister (nametag misspelled)!! The cut-and-pasted note didn't say,

"Merry Christmas from Santa," as it had in previous years; it simply read, "I know WHERE you have been sleeping."!

I couldn't even move. I don't know who was more shocked, her or me. David just took it in stride; but then again, ignorance is bliss. Now this was scary! She thought it had been someone in Twentynine Palms, as had I...but now, I truly did not know what to think!

Who could have found me? *How* did they find me? The one constant thing throughout all those years is the fact that whoever was behind this wonderful Christmas magic had a lot of information about me – and those around me – that was not common knowledge. The only person other than myself that would have had access to places, times, addresses, company, etc. was me, or perhaps the guests themselves. I would like to note here however, that even the guests themselves changed throughout the years. The mystery of Our Santa...our Angel continued to grow in its magic and mystery.

And my new investigator? Did he believe?

When I returned to work and related the events of my San Jose trip, I found him speechless for the very first time. He sat and listened to every detail, his face reflecting complete and total astonishment. He asked a question or two, but after that day, we never spoke about it again.

Christmas, 1988 was short and sweet.

Amy was spending Christmas in San Jose with her Aunt and because of the holiday schedule at work it was impossible for us to make the trip. Matthew was still in South Carolina working, and that left David and me at home.

Christmas fell on a Sunday this year. On Saturday December 24th in with our mail I found a legal size envelope addressed to me, but it had no return address. The stamp had been cancelled, but the point of origin was so blurry it was un-readable.

When I opened the envelope, I found letters cut and pasted on a piece of paper, which read, "Merry Christmas from Santa." Also in the envelope were *four* $100 Stater Brothers gift certificates made out to me. YEAH!!!! Finally! Something tangible to track...*I had a clue!* How hard would it be to simply call Stater Brothers and find out who purchased these certificates?

Bizarre though it may sound, when the records were pulled up on the computer, the registered purchaser's name was *S. Clause!* The store manager then called the main office and after several minutes a very bewildered office manager gave us the following information: There was no purchase point of origin listed on the file. The purchaser was listed as S. Clause, 1988 N. Pole St., Elfkin, Alaska. (And yes, I did check! There is *no* such place as Elfkin, Alaska)*

I next went to the post office to see if perhaps they could determine where the post mark originated. I hoped against hope that maybe some kind of code also appeared within the cancellation that would provide some information. Once again, all roads led nowhere.

NOTE: Several days after the initial inquiry the local store manager called to tell me that his contact at the main office had tried to find the person who sold the certificates. No one even remembered such a transaction!

Christmas, 1989. I can say – without a doubt – that 1989 was a year that I never want to repeat! It's almost as if there were a measure of hardships that still needed to transpire, and for some reason they were all encapsulated into that one year.

By the end of the year, I seemed to be estranged from my two oldest children and in a precarious state with my youngest son.

Amy married a man who brought three young children from a previous marriage with him. The oldest child was 5 and the youngest was 6 months old. The children were no strangers to me. He and I attended the same church. I knew that he was working a full time job and being "Mr. Mom," too. I occasionally babysat the kids so he could have some free time. In fact, that's how he and Amy met. Amy had come home from college for the weekend and was at the house when he came to pick up the kids. They started "courting" shortly after, and about a year later, were married. They had been married about a year and a half when things between Amy and me became strained. Slowly, the situation deteriorated to the point of alienation. The curious thing was the fact that we never argued. (I was to find out much later that Amy's feelings were related to the problems I was having with David.)

Matthew was just caught up in circumstances. The situation between Amy and I had gotten to the point where Matthew felt compelled to declare his loyalties, and...he had "pitched his tent in the enemy camp." So, I lost another ally.

All three kids were spending time away, and I began to feel very left out. It was as though I was being pushed out of the family. At the same time, I was becoming very concerned about changes I saw in David. I tried getting Amy and Matthew's thoughts and feelings about David's behavior, but the more I asked, the more vague they became. None of us realized what was happening. David was definitely changing. He had become somewhat withdrawn and secretive with me. His happy-go-lucky demeanor soon gave way to moodiness and argument. We were all motivated by a genuine desire to help David, and in love, each of us

in our own way were trying to "rescue" him. Finally I asked that we all have a meeting, Amy, Matthew, and I all sat down to see if we could work together instead of against each other. That's when it became apparent that each of us was trying to blame everyone else for whatever was wrong. David didn't need saving; he needed help!

In August, I went on a one week retreat to Glorietta, New Mexico. David didn't want to go; he wanted to stay with Amy and her family while I was away. It was the first time I had ever been on a vacation, and I was a little hesitant to leave David behind. I went back and forth between going and not going. Finally, two days before leaving, I decided to take the trip.

It was a wonderful week! The weather couldn't have been better. I had heard that New Mexico was famous for its scenery and beautiful skies, but I wasn't prepared for just how lovely it was. In all my life I have never seen the sky such a rich, dark blue. The clouds were huge, and hung in the sky like new cotton. The mountains were alive with wild flowers, and the air smelled like sweet lilac. By the end of the week I had almost forgotten the problems I had left behind.

On the way home, however, my mind left the solitude of that retreat and turned to thoughts of home. I was going to make some changes in my life! I wanted to take a more active part in David's life. I worked nights, he was in school in the day, and we didn't see a great deal of each other. This also left him home alone much of the time. Even though he was 16, I thought maybe he needed a parent to be there when he needed one. (I was also looking forward to painting the inside of the house and doing some redecorating.)

I had gone to Glorietta with several friends, and we all took our turn driving. I had finished my turn and now it was time for me to be a passenger. I had plenty of time to think as the car traveled quietly through the night. I felt refreshed and the feeling of helplessness that I felt on the way, was now a feeling of determination. I was going to face whatever was ahead and mend whatever tensions might still exist between my children and myself. The more I pondered the events of the past several months, the more I could see that not only had each of the children distanced themselves from me, but also from each other. Now things were starting to fit into place. I could see what had happened; I just needed to find out how to "fix" it. I was resolved to make us a *family* again.

I was delighted with my new found confidence. I had always been a person who ran away from trouble of any kind. Now I wasn't going to run away, I was going to face it, and to the best of my ability, resolve it. As my confidence grew, a feeling of peace came over me. As our car moved quietly through the night, I drifted into a quiet peaceful sleep, lulled by the sound of the highway. The peace was not to last however.

I awoke with a terrible pain in my chest. I couldn't catch my breath, and I felt a tremendous weight on my chest. The pain in my left arm was almost unbearable. One look at me and the driver signaled the others in our caravan to stop. Our journey home turned into a high speed race to the nearest hospital. It was determined in the emergency room that I had had a mild heart attack, so I was admitted. It was not until several days later that I was discharged from the Kingman, Arizona hospital.

When I finally returned home it was mutually decided by David and me that he would remain with Amy while I recuperated. By this time I was already committed to being out for work for two months until I would get a doctor's release to return. In addition to trying to heal physically, I now faced a new emotional and financial predicament.

When I finally returned to work the last week in November, David had returned home and the scheduled court date was the first week of December. Things were dismal, to say the least. Even if I won the court case, the money lost while I was ill and the money I had paid the attorney left a zero balance of funds. The Christmas situation was very much as it had been the first year "Our Santa" came. The only bright spot was having to provide for only one child.

Sunday the 3rd of December started off very routinely. David and I had gone to church. As usual, we attended the early morning service, then Sunday School. I also did "Children's Time," which necessitated me staying about 15 minutes into the second service. David typically waited for me in the back row of the sanctuary, and when I was finished, we left together. That Sunday, when we left the building I realized I had forgotten my Bible in the nursery area. I sent David to the car to wait while I went back to get it.

When I came back out of the church, I was surprised to see David walking towards me in the parking lot. He asked me what all the "stuff" in the car was. I explained that I had gathered up the nursery linen to take home and launder. He got a very peculiar look on his face and asked simply, "Gift wrapped?" I suppose I thought he was kidding me, or maybe it was a sarcastic response. I really didn't give the conversation much thought. As I got into the car, however, I couldn't miss the two gifts tied together on the front seat: one rather large one wrapped in bright, shiny red paper; the other about the size of a two-pound box of See's Candy.

Now, the town of Twentynine Palms has several very active service organizations, most of which sell See's Candy for fund raising. Needless to say, at Christmas time, 2 lbs. of See's is a *very* popular (and not unusual) gift! After I got into the car, I began to inspect the packages. It was very unnerving to find the piece of paper with letters cut from magazines, glued and taped on it. The note simply said, *"To Nell, Open A.S.A.P. Merry Christmas."*

My first thought was, *"Our Santa!,"* but it was too early in the season. Besides, one of the boxes was wrapped in pink paper and my birthday was in a week and a half. I kept thinking, "It couldn't be Our Santa, or *could* it?"

The next dilemma was the *A.S.A.P.* .. Did it mean as soon as possible now, or as soon as possible Christmas day? I didn't want to spoil a Christmas surprise, but on the other hand, if the gifts were something that would spoil in three weeks, which would be a shame. I just couldn't make up my mind. What should I do? I shook, squeezed, sniffed, and probed the boxes hoping for some direction. *No clue!*

Finally, David asked me if I was going to open the packages. I shared my dilemma with him and he had the perfect solution: I could open the packages and if we needed to do something with the contents we could; if not, we could re-wrap them and put them under the Christmas tree and open them first on Christmas Day. It was a great idea! Why I didn't think of that!?

I opened the smaller box, the one wrapped with pink paper. As I unfolded the tissue I saw a typed 3 x 5 card. It read: "Psalms 37:4 Take delight in the Lord and he will give you the desires of your heart." Under the next fold of tissue I found two round trip plane tickets to my sister's for Christmas through New Year's Day! One ticket for David and one ticket for me. Needless to say, it took several minutes for me to compose myself. I was totally shocked...I didn't know what to think. David was speechless.

When I opened the other gift, I found, of course...a set of towels with a $5.00 bill a $20.00 bill and another note that simply said, "from Santa."

EPILOGUE

Over the years I have tried to find out who the most wonderful "Our Santa" was. I thought surely the last year would be easy to trace. I called the airline, only to find – as in prior years – all leads led to nowhere.

Calling the airline carrier for the origin of the ticket was really interesting, though, and for awhile I thought this might be the end of my search. The "paper trail" zigzagged between five different travel agencies throughout California and even one in Arizona! The outcome was that the tickets had been purchased in my name and paid for with cash. Again, *nobody* remembered those specific transactions!

Throughout our seven Christmases, the only commonalities were the gifts for the kids and me: the towels, the money, and other gifts that were tailored for each of us, and of course the cut-and-pasted notes.

Each year our address, friends, Christmas guests, color preference, sizes, and circumstances changed. Each year there were things that only I would know about. For instance, the year Matthew got to come home from the hospital for Christmas I only found out the afternoon of the 23rd. I didn't talk to anyone except the agencies which would provide the hospital equipment. And my personal gifts over the years were almost always in my favorite color, periwinkle. Definitely not a common color! Coincidence? Maybe...but, *seven years* of coincidence?

In 1897 a young Virginia O'Hanlon wrote to the *New York Sun*, asking if there really was a Santa Claus. In his legendary editorial response, Francis Church sagely replied: "Yes Virginia, there is a Santa Claus ... Not believe in Santa Claus? You might as well not believe in fairies...No Santa Claus! Thank God, he lives, and he lives forever." I believe that wise man knew what many people know, but are often unwilling to admit: miracles happen when people believe! Some may quibble about "Santa Claus" as the source of those miracles, but I think Mr. Church got it right. The timelessness of giving and the heart of giving are undeniable.

The Sun.

TUESDAY, SEPTEMBER 21, 1897.

Yes, Virginia, Ther Is A Santa Claus

Remember that first Christmas of ours, when I had no hope and sat alone in the dark living room? I remember the deep despair I felt and then, that mysterious light...seeing the Nativity and suddenly knowing what Christmas was really about. And angels? The Bible tells us about Michael and Gabriel. Why couldn't there be an angel named *Santa*? The Reverend Billy Graham wrote a book titled, *Angels: God's Secret Agents*. In the book, Rev. Graham tells how God primarily uses people to accomplish his tasks, but sometimes a person just won't do. God then dispatches one of his angels to perform the mission. Magic? Maybe... but, more like a Christmas miracle – because what God does is far more than magic.

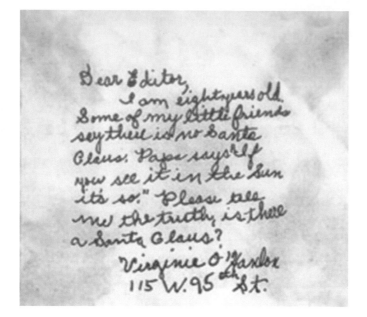

Is There a Santa Claus?

We take pleasure in answering at once and thus prominently the communication below, expressing at the same time our great gratification that its faithful author is numbered among the friends of THE SUN:

"DEAR EDITOR: I am 8 years old.

"Some of my little friends say there is no Santa Claus.

"Papa says 'If you see it in THE SUN it's so.'

"Please tell me the truth; is there a Santa Claus?

"VIRGINIA O'HANLON.

"115 WEST NINETY-FIFTH STREET."

VIRGINIA, your little friends are wrong. They have been affected by the skepticism of a skeptical age. They do not believe except they see. They think that nothing can be which is not comprehensible by their little minds. All minds, VIRGINIA, whether they be men's or children's, are little. In this great universe of ours man is a mere insect, an ant, in his intellect, as compared with the boundless world about him, as measured by the intelligence capable of grasping the whole of truth and knowledge.

Yes, VIRGINIA, there is a Santa Claus. He exists as certainly as love and generosity and devotion exist, and you know that they abound and give to your life its highest beauty and joy. Alas! how dreary would be the world if there were no Santa Claus. It would be as dreary as if there were no VIRGINIAS. There would be no childlike faith then, no poetry, no romance to make tolerable this existence. We should have no enjoyment, except in sense and sight. The eternal light with which childhood fills the world would be extinguished.

Not believe in Santa Claus! You might as well not believe in fairies! You might get your papa to hire men to watch in all the chimneys on Christmas Eve to catch Santa Claus, but even if they did not see Santa Claus coming down, what would that prove? Nobody sees Santa Claus, but that is no sign that there is no Santa Claus. The most real things in the world are those that neither children nor men can see. Did you ever see fairies dancing on the lawn? Of course not, but that's no proof that they are not there. Nobody can conceive or imagine all the wonders there are unseen and unseeable in the world.

You may tear apart the baby's rattle and see what makes the noise inside, but there is a veil covering the unseen world which not the strongest man, nor even the united strength of all the strongest men that ever lived, could tear apart. Only faith, fancy, poetry, love, romance, can push aside that curtain and view and picture the supernal beauty and glory beyond. Is it all real? Ah, VIRGINIA, in all this world there is nothing else real and abiding.

No Santa Claus! Thank GOD! he lives, and he lives forever. A thousand years from now, VIRGINIA, nay, ten times ten thousand years from now, he will continue to make glad the heart of childhood.

All I know for sure is, "Yes, Virginia, there is a Santa Claus!" It was true then, and it's true now. But now I know, too, that Someone bigger and more powerful than "Santa Claus" makes miracles happen... miracles that feel like magic but are undeniably Heaven-sent...just like *"Our Santa Angel."*

About the Author

Nell is a retired library specialist who lives is a small desert town in so. Calif. She is a divorced mom who successfully raised 3 children on her own. She has a great sense of humor. There's almost nothing she can't do with her hands. She crochets, knits, quilts, bakes & sews as well as tailoring. Probably the thing she loved doing the most was creating all kinds of greeting cards through the stamping media. She was even commissioned by another town to make "thank you" cards for their chamber of commerce.

These days *Nell* is enjoying retirement and spending time with 7 grandchildren and 7 great grandchildren. Nell has a great love for the Lord. During the hardest times in her life she never wavered in the belief in God and His ever presence in her life.

Printed in the United States
By Bookmasters